kids draw

ANGELS, ELVES, FAIRIES & MORE

CHRISTOPHER HART

WATSON-GUPTILL PUBLICATIONS/
NEW YORK

For Isabella

Senior Editor: Candace Raney
Editors: Alisa Palazzo and Julie Mazur
Designers: Bob Fillie, Graphiti Design, Inc. and Cheryl Viker
Production Manager: Hector Campbell

First published in 2001 by
Watson-Guptill Publications,
a division of BPI Communications, Inc.,
770 Broadway, New York, N.Y. 10003
www.watsonguptill.com

Based on *How to Draw Fantasy Characters,* first
published by Watson-Guptill Publications in 1999.

Library of Congress Card Number: 00-111762

Printed in Singapore

First printing, 2001

1 2 3 4 5 6 7 8 / 08 07 06 05 04 03 02 01

CONTENTS

INTRODUCTION

Kids are so lucky! They get to pore over storybooks filled with unicorns and mermaids, genies, fairies, and more. What do grownups get to read? *The Wall Street Journal.* Luckily, cartoonists never have to grow up. They get to draw these cool characters all the time. And so can you, with the help of this book!

All of your favorite fantasy characters are here, from fairy godmothers to Hercules, from Pegasus to elves and gnomes. Before you know it, mythology and magic will be flowing from your pencil.

Remember these pointers as you learn to draw each character: Try not to press too hard on your pencil. Draw with long, sweeping lines rather than short, choppy ones. And don't draw too small. Your drawings are important—let them fill the page!

Fantasy characters live in a world of wonder and magic, but none so wonderful as your imagination. With it, you can make something terrific. I just know it! Your pencil is your ticket to a fantastic voyage. Are you ready to set sail? Then let's go!

SEA CREATURES

Sea creatures are perhaps the most mysterious fantasy characters. This is because they are the most fleeting. As soon as you spot one, it dives out of site, vanishing into the deep.

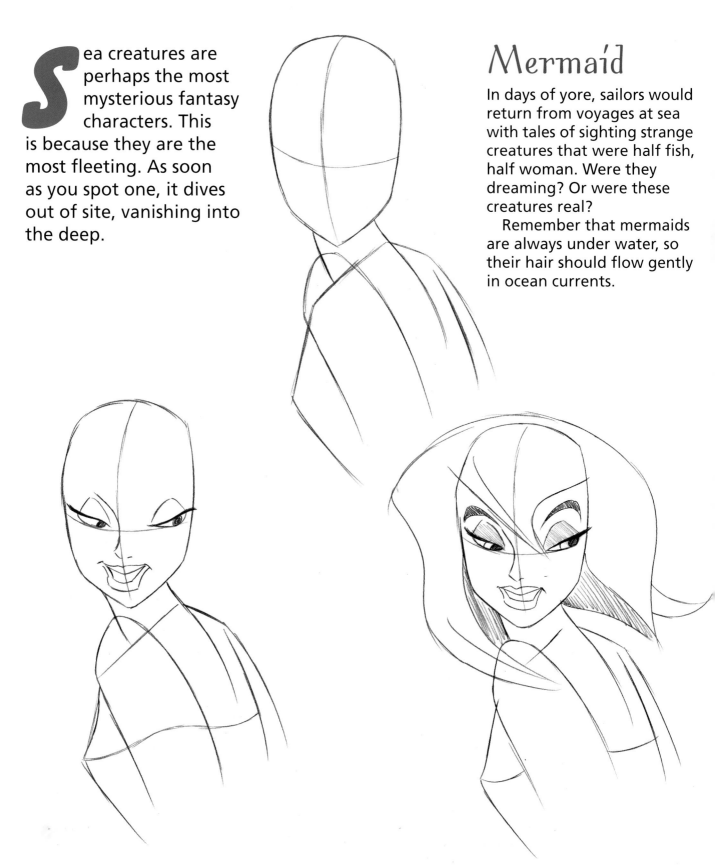

Mermaid

In days of yore, sailors would return from voyages at sea with tales of sighting strange creatures that were half fish, half woman. Were they dreaming? Or were these creatures real?

Remember that mermaids are always under water, so their hair should flow gently in ocean currents.

The Mermaid Body

Mermaids twist and turn as they glide through the water. Their tail fins flap up and down as they swim.

The law of *perspective* says that forms closer to you will look larger than forms farther away. So in this pose, the mermaid's body should get bigger as it comes toward you.

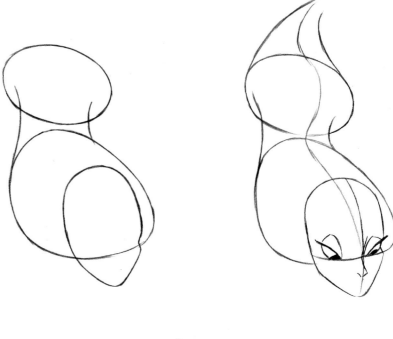

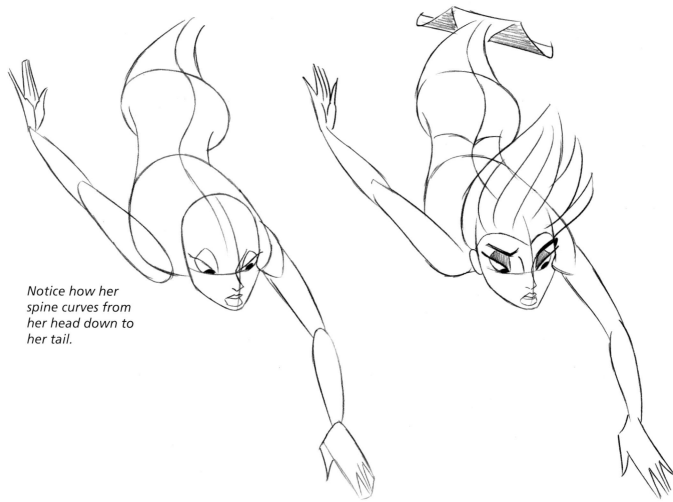

Notice how her spine curves from her head down to her tail.

Mermaid Poses

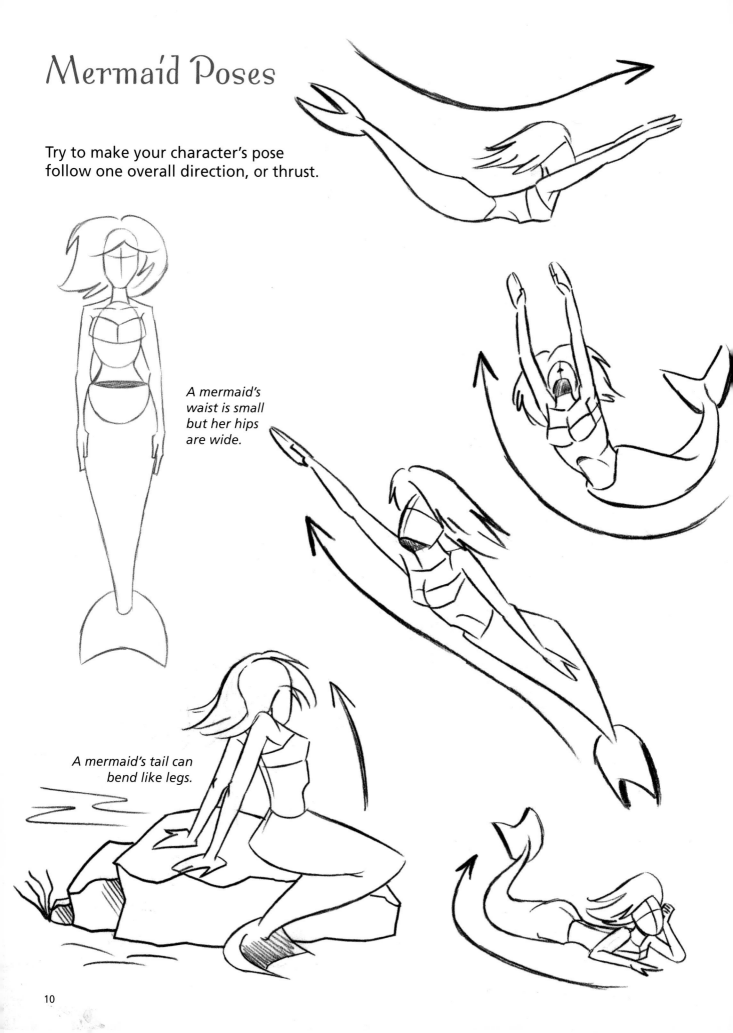

Try to make your character's pose follow one overall direction, or thrust.

A mermaid's waist is small but her hips are wide.

A mermaid's tail can bend like legs.

Merman Walking His Merdog

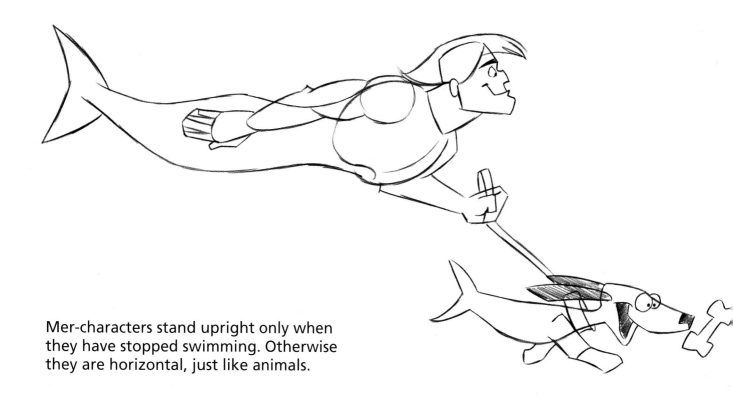

Mer-characters stand upright only when they have stopped swimming. Otherwise they are horizontal, just like animals.

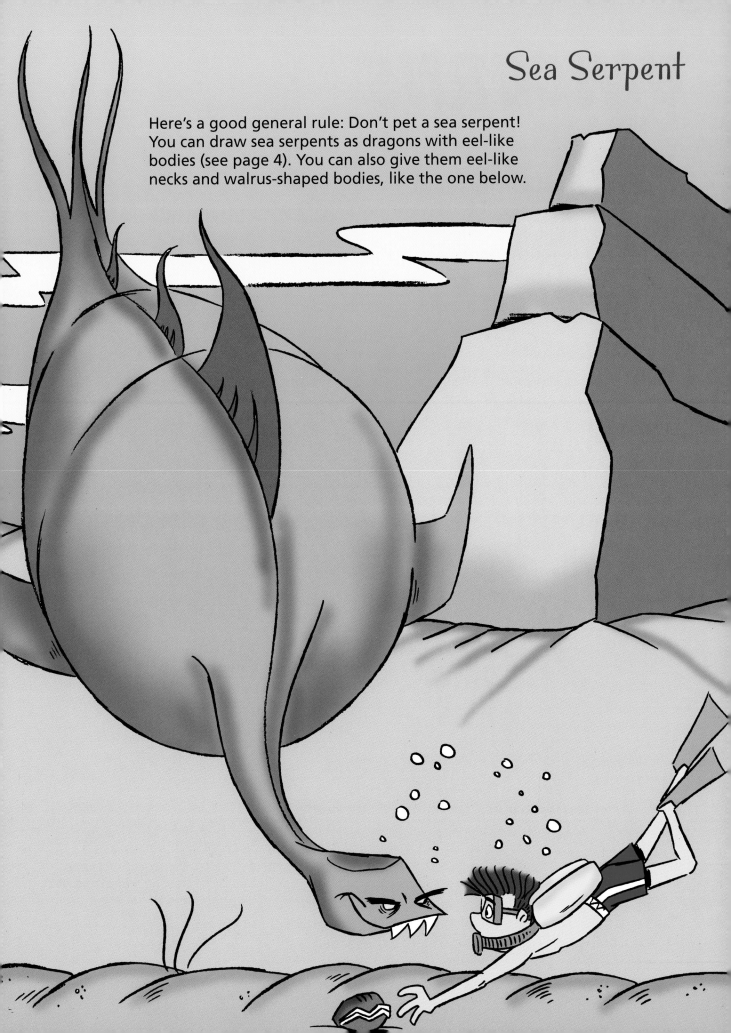

Sea Serpent

Here's a good general rule: Don't pet a sea serpent! You can draw sea serpents as dragons with eel-like bodies (see page 4). You can also give them eel-like necks and walrus-shaped bodies, like the one below.

UNICORNS

What is a unicorn? Is it just a horse with a horn? Yes, it is that. But it is also magic, legend, and so much more!

The Head

The head of a unicorn is like that of a horse. It must be strong, yet graceful and beautiful. Let's start with the profile.

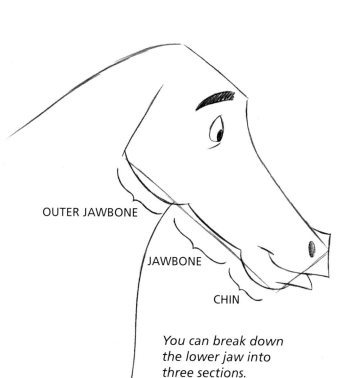

OUTER JAWBONE

JAWBONE

CHIN

You can break down the lower jaw into three sections.

The horn and a long, flowing mane make the unicorn different from an ordinary horse.

Add a pattern to the horn so it looks magical, not plain.

ADDING THE HORN

RIGHT
The horn goes on the forehead . . .

WRONG
. . . *not* on the bridge of the nose.

Front View

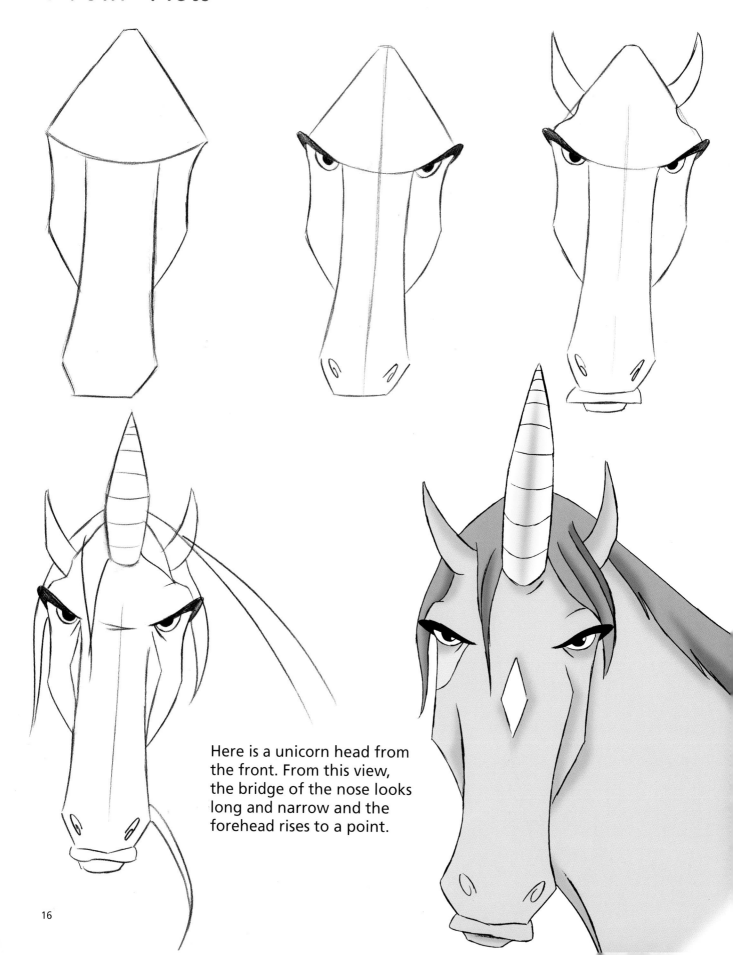

Here is a unicorn head from the front. From this view, the bridge of the nose looks long and narrow and the forehead rises to a point.

The 3/4 view can be tricky. Only a tiny part of the far side of the face should poke out from behind the bridge of the nose.

Notice that you can draw a unicorn's mane neatly styled (left), or with the front piece curled around the horn (below).

The Unicorn Body

MALE
The male unicorn has sturdy legs and a forceful stance. Legend has it that unicorns were fearless fighters. They were prized for their horns, which were said to be magical.

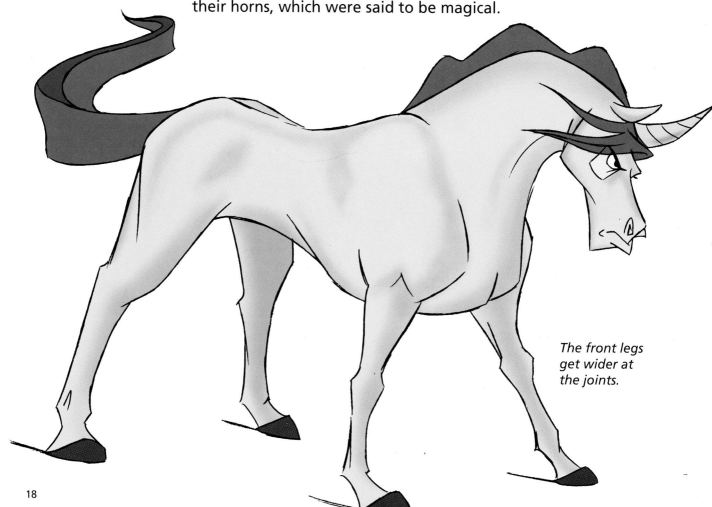

The front legs get wider at the joints.

FEMALE

The female unicorn has a fancy mane and tail. Her legs taper to small hooves, but she is still strong, athletic, and brave.

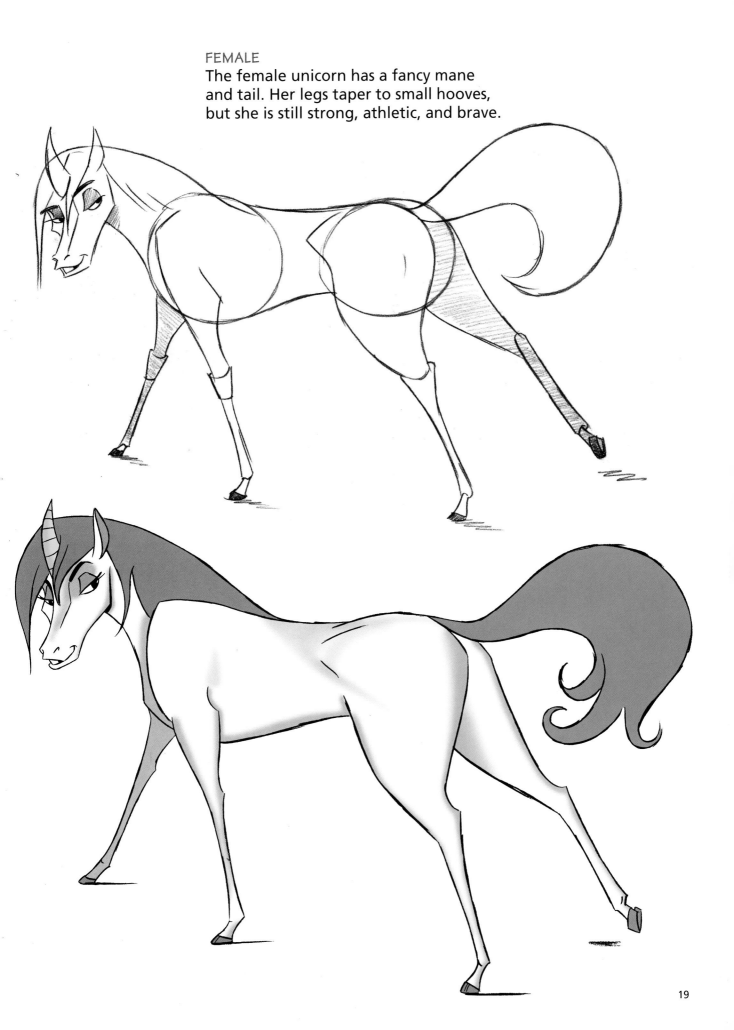

The Young Unicorn

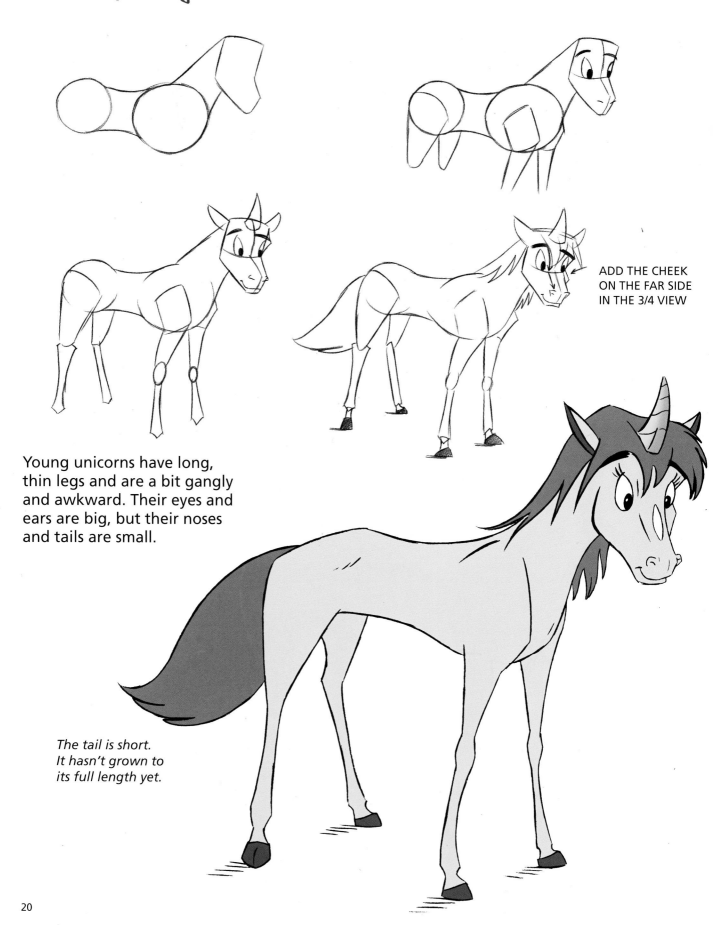

ADD THE CHEEK
ON THE FAR SIDE
IN THE 3/4 VIEW

Young unicorns have long, thin legs and are a bit gangly and awkward. Their eyes and ears are big, but their noses and tails are small.

The tail is short. It hasn't grown to its full length yet.

Young Unicorn Expressions

Young characters have rounder faces, which you can stretch and squash to show many kinds of emotions.

SURPRISE

UNCERTAINTY

DISDAIN

PLEASING THOUGHT

GLEE

HAPPINESS

DISAPPOINTMENT

MYTHOLOGICAL FIGURES

Stories from Greek and Roman mythology feature all sorts of colorful characters. Many are gods and demigods, and all have special powers.

Zeus

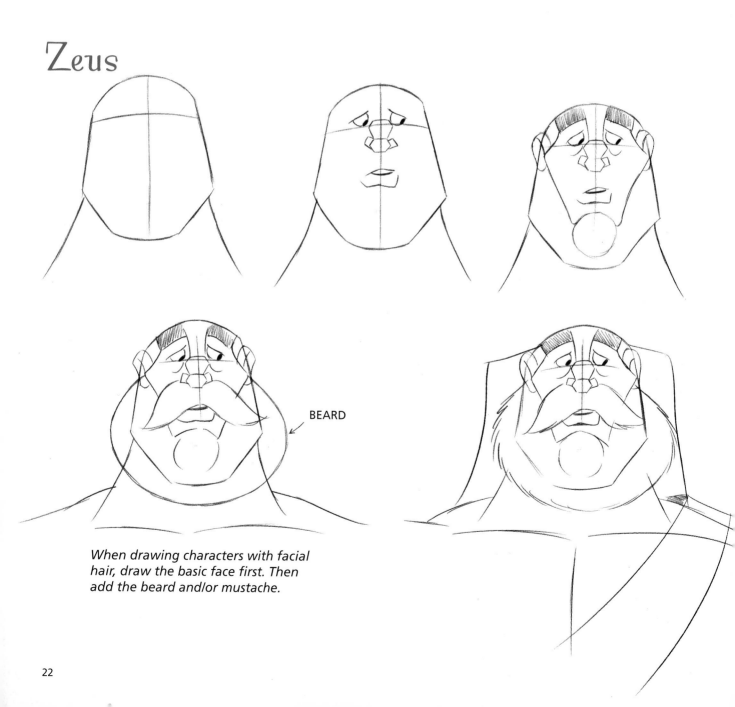

BEARD

When drawing characters with facial hair, draw the basic face first. Then add the beard and/or mustache.

Awesome. Mighty. Commanding. Emotional. These are the words that come to mind when thinking of Zeus, king of the Greek gods.

Zeus Enthroned

According to Greek mythology, Zeus' throne is on Mount Olympus, home of the Greek gods. From high among the clouds, Zeus can see everything that happens on Earth.

Sketch the entire figure first, even if part of it will be hidden in the final drawing.

A NOTE ABOUT CLOUDS
Bumpy clouds with flat
bottoms are best for
fantasy drawings. Clouds
that are bumpy all around
look too cartoony.

Neptune

Neptune is the Roman god of the sea. He is strong, bearded, and wise. He carries a trident and wears a crown. His robe billows in the water.

The Cyclops

The cyclops' head is based on just a simple shape—the oval. But it still looks awesome!

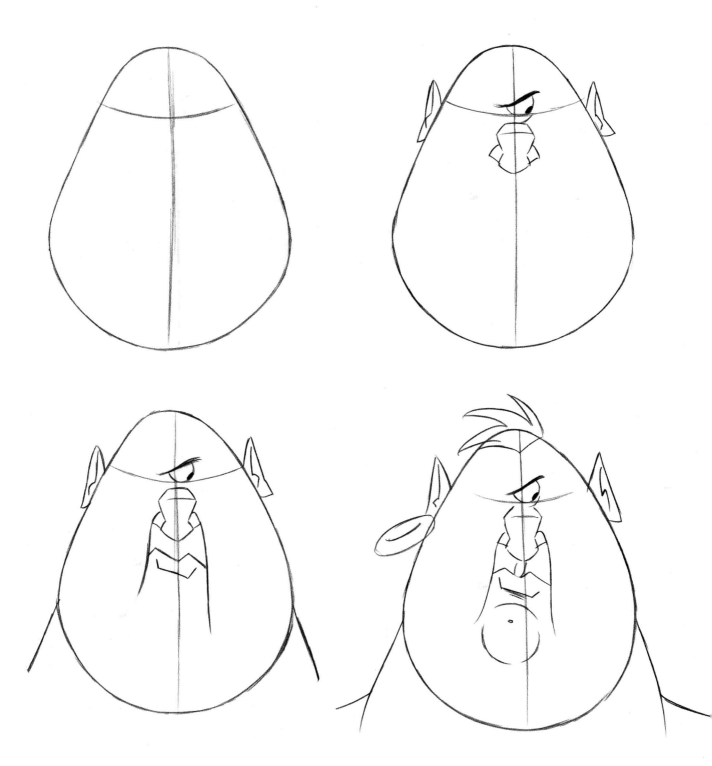

A cyclops is an evil creature with only one eye. He's also a giant, shown here by his huge jaw and neck. I've given him pointed ears and an animal skin to make him look meaner.

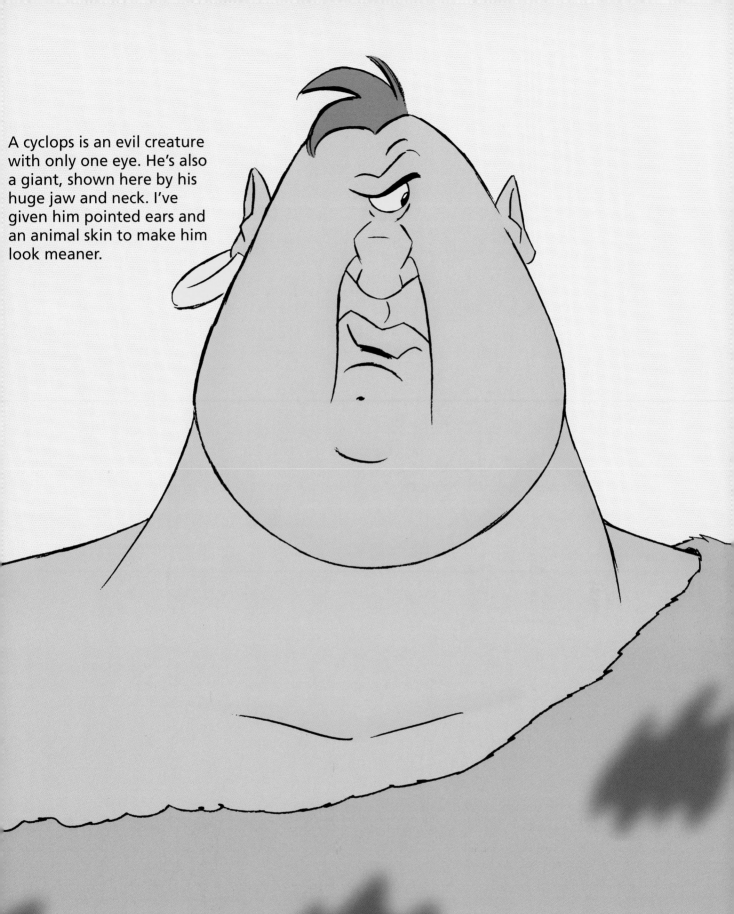

The Cyclops Body

Notice the angles of the calf muscles and ankle bones.

The body of a cyclops gets smaller toward the head and shoulders. This is because of *perspective*: The farther away something is, the smaller it appears. The head dips below the shoulders to give him a brutish look.

Hercules

Hercules was the original strongman. He has a thick neck that widens into broad shoulders.

This guy gives heavy lifting a whole new meaning!

Pan

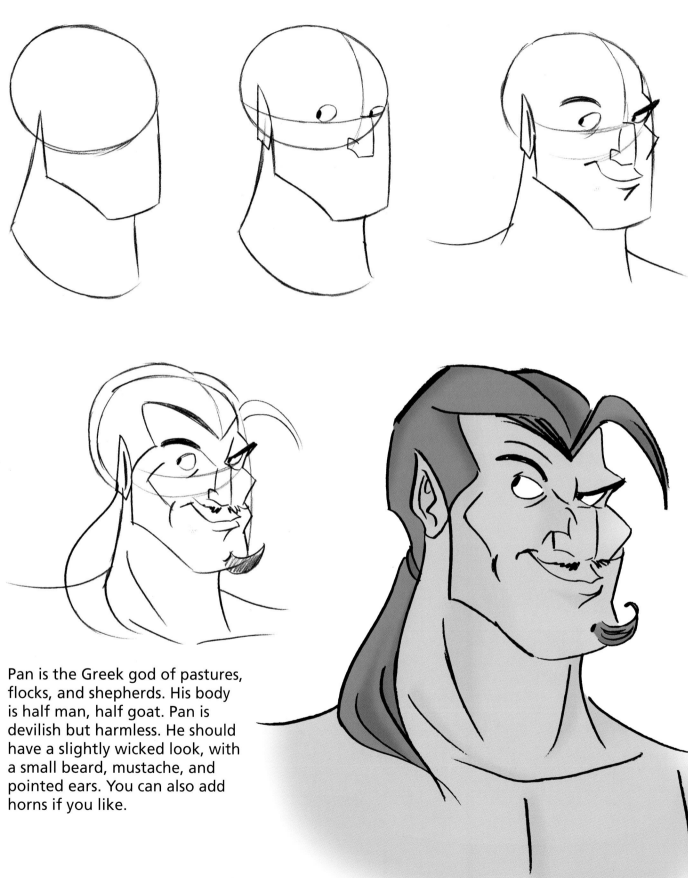

Pan is the Greek god of pastures, flocks, and shepherds. His body is half man, half goat. Pan is devilish but harmless. He should have a slightly wicked look, with a small beard, mustache, and pointed ears. You can also add horns if you like.

The knee is a point where two joints meet. This creates two small bumps.

A bone sticks out here.

THE LEGS OF A GOAT
Unlike the centaur (page 40), who has horse legs, Pan has the legs of a goat.

Pan Courting a Maiden

In this scene, Pan courts a maiden by playing music for her on his Pan flute, an instrument named for him.

   Notice how the mountains overlap one another and how the brook zigzags into the distance to create a feeling of depth.

Pegasus

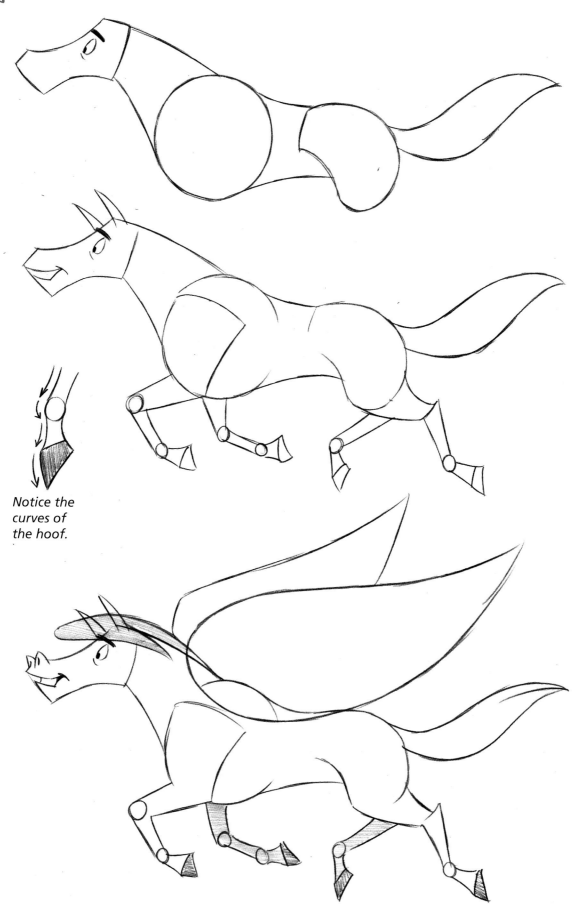

Notice the curves of the hoof.

Pegasus is a horse with wings.
When flying, he should always
be in mid-gallop. His wings
must be large enough to keep
his body in the air.

The Centaur

The centaur is half man, half horse. He's powerful and pretty strange looking.

The Female Centaur

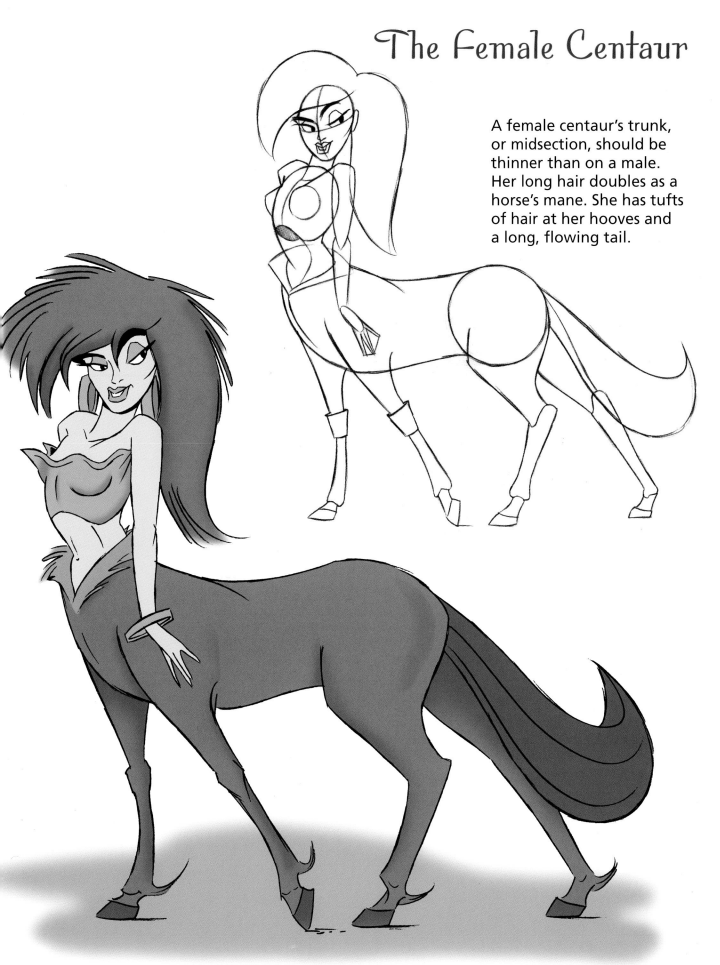

A female centaur's trunk, or midsection, should be thinner than on a male. Her long hair doubles as a horse's mane. She has tufts of hair at her hooves and a long, flowing tail.

Cupid

Cupid is the Roman god of love. When he hits people with his arrows, they fall in love, although sometimes he hits the wrong person! Cupid is always drawn as a baby. His arms and legs should be short and chubby. His head should be large in relation to his body.

Cupid Expressions

Cupid has all sorts of emotions. Here are a few for you to practice.

HIT THE WRONG TARGET!

BULL'S-EYE!

THINKING

ANGRY

EMBARRASSED

WATCHING

GENIES, ANGELS, AND FAIRIES

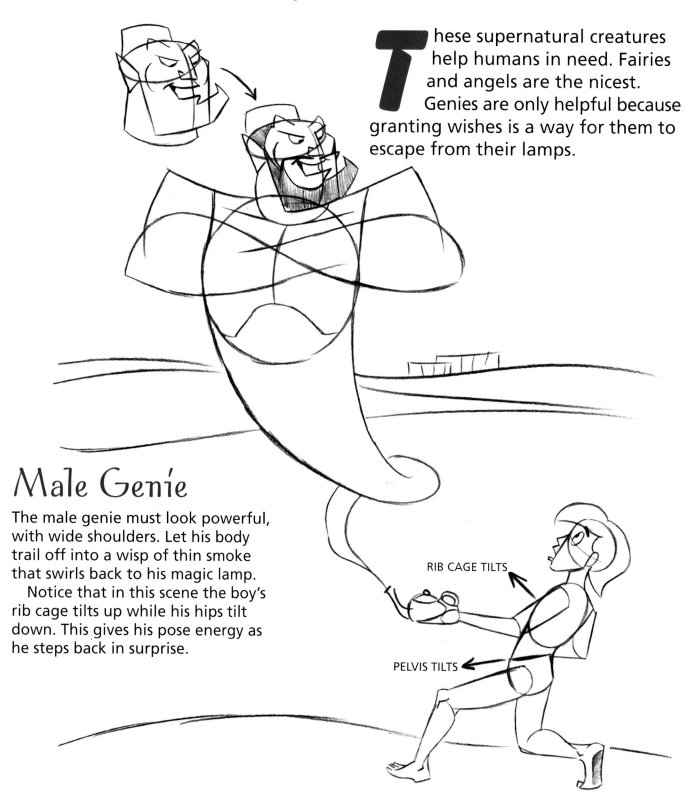

These supernatural creatures help humans in need. Fairies and angels are the nicest. Genies are only helpful because granting wishes is a way for them to escape from their lamps.

Male Genie

The male genie must look powerful, with wide shoulders. Let his body trail off into a wisp of thin smoke that swirls back to his magic lamp.

Notice that in this scene the boy's rib cage tilts up while his hips tilt down. This gives his pose energy as he steps back in surprise.

RIB CAGE TILTS

PELVIS TILTS

Female Genie

The beautiful female genie is mischievous—she is neither good nor evil. Give her a high ponytail, huge round earrings, and magical eyes.

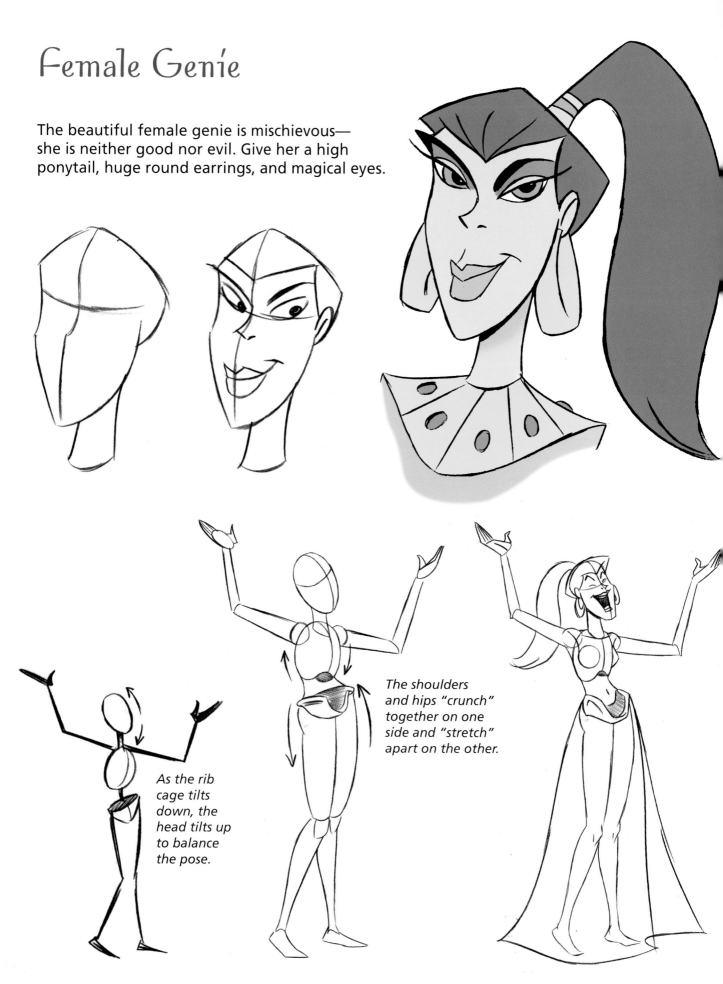

As the rib cage tilts down, the head tilts up to balance the pose.

The shoulders and hips "crunch" together on one side and "stretch" apart on the other.

Guardian Angel

The guardian angel is like a caring, kind grandfather. Give him a cane or umbrella and a twinkle in his eye. Remember to always draw the body first, then add the clothing.

Notice the pear-shaped body.

Fairy Godmother

A fairy godmother appears when a heroine is desperate and has nowhere else to turn. She is a plump, kind grandmotherly type. Give her a long flowing dress, cape, and a tall sorcerer's hat. And a magic wand never hurts, either.

The Tooth Fairy

The tooth fairy always appears quietly in the middle of the night. Notice how the tilt of her head makes her seem gentle and loving.

CIRCLE OF INTEREST

This is where the main parts of a drawing come together. It keeps the reader's eye moving in a circle, from one important element to the next. Your eye goes from the tooth fairy's head, to her hand, to the little girl, to the fairy's other arm, and then back to the fairy's head.

Fairy Princess

The fairy princess is the size of a butterfly. Kind and shy, she tries to help people in trouble.

The only "big people" fairy princesses trust are young girls. Young girls won't betray them by telling grown-ups about their existence.

LITTLE FOLK

Little people live in a tiny world. To them, a chair leg is a giant tree. They are experts at hiding, and they work together to survive.

Elves

Elves are tiny, magical creatures. Their heads, hands, and feet are large, and their clothes should be loose. They have pointed noses, long pointed ears, and large mouths. Their eyes should be thin and pointed as well.

The Elf Habitat

Elves live on the forest floor, among blades of grass, dandelions, and mushrooms. Tree trunks serve as their homes. A huge harvest for an elf is a single acorn, which can feed an entire elfin family for weeks.

Gnomes

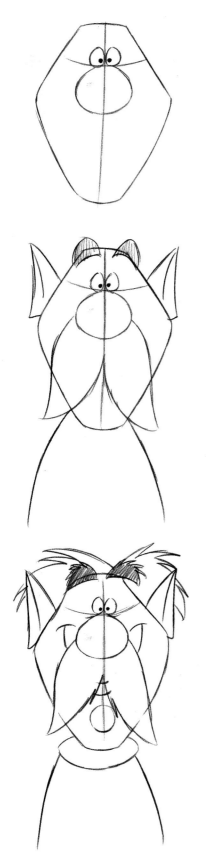

Gnomes are like elves, but more human looking. They are also usually older—like little old men. Gnomes have rounded noses, not pointy ones like elves. And only gnomes have mustaches, beards, or glasses.

The Gnome Body

Gnomes are harder working
than elves. They're always doing
chores. This one is wearing a
snazzy vest and turtleneck.

Leprechauns

If you catch a leprechaun, he will lead you to his pot of gold. But it's nearly impossible to catch one! Leprechauns are clever and very tricky. The one I caught talked me into letting him go. Next time, I'll be more careful.

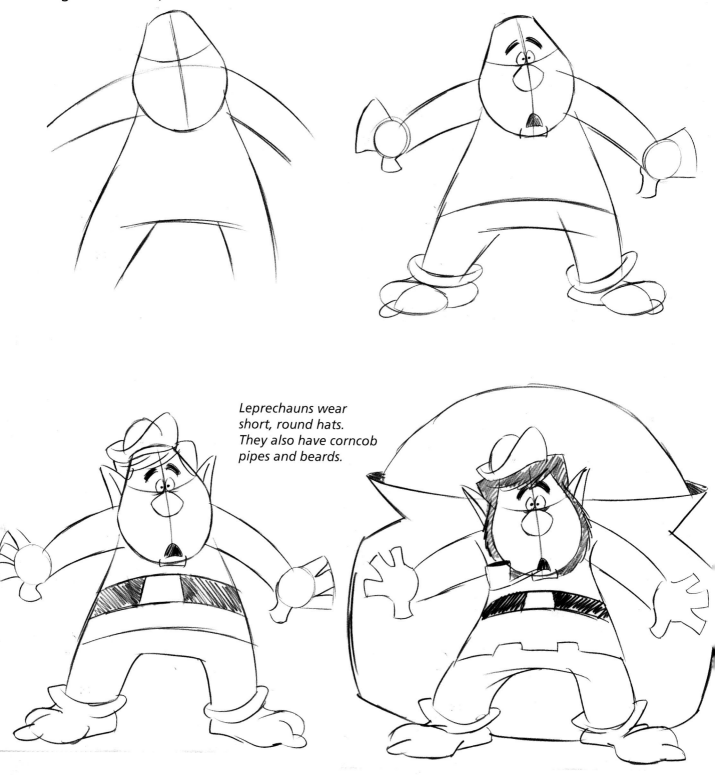

Leprechauns wear short, round hats. They also have corncob pipes and beards.

"Little People"

When you draw tiny people, put familiar, "giant-sized" props in the background to make them look small. Little people are always in a hurry to find hiding spots—being seen means risking capture!

This is called a thumbnail sketch. It is a quick, small sketch that lays out the scene. Once you're happy with the thumbnail, you can draw the scene in more detail.

INDEX